FREE DVD

MW00329505

Essential Test Tips DVD from Trivium Test Prep

Dear Customer,

Thank you for purchasing from Cirrus Test Prep! Whether you're looking to join the military, get into college, or advance your career, we're honored to be a part of your journey.

To show our appreciation (and to help you relieve a little of that test-prep stress), we're offering a **FREE *CBEST Essential Test Tips DVD**** by Cirrus Test Prep. Our DVD includes 35 test preparation strategies that will help keep you calm and collected before and during your big exam. All we ask is that you email us your feedback and describe your experience with our product. Amazing, awful, or just so-so: we want to hear what you have to say!

To receive your **FREE *CBEST Essential Test Tips DVD***, please email us at 5star@cirrustestprep.com. Include "Free 5 Star" in the subject line and the following information in your email:

1. The title of the product you purchased.
2. Your rating from 1 – 5 (with 5 being the best).
3. Your feedback about the product, including how our materials helped you meet your goals and ways in which we can improve our products.
4. Your full name and shipping address so we can send your **FREE *CBEST Essential Test Tips DVD***.

If you have any questions or concerns please feel free to contact us directly at 5star@cirrustestprep.com. Thank you, and good luck with your studies!

* Please note that the free DVD is <u>not included</u> with this book. To receive the free DVD, please follow the instructions above.

CBEST Flash Cards

CBEST TEST PREP REVIEW WITH 300+ FLASH CARDS FOR THE CALIFORNIA BASIC EDUCATIONAL SKILLS TEST

Table of Contents

Introduction i

Reading.. 1

Writing...79

Mathematics 147

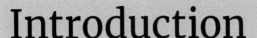

Introduction

Congratulations on choosing to take the California Basic Educational Skills Test (CBEST)! By purchasing this book, you've taken the first step toward becoming a teacher, an enriching and satisfying career.

This guide will provide you with a detailed overview of the California Basic Educational Skills Test (CBEST) so you know exactly what to expect on test day. It will prepare you for all three of the sections: the Reading section, the Mathematics section, and the Writing section. We'll take you through all the concepts covered on these tests and give you the opportunity to test your knowledge with practice questions. Even if it's been a while since you last took a major test, don't worry; we'll make sure you're more than ready!

WHAT IS THE CALIFORNIA BASIC EDUCATIONAL SKILLS TEST (CBEST)?

The CBEST is used in the state of California to measure teacher candidates' aptitude in mathematics, reading, language skills, and writing. You may take the sections individually on separate dates, or you may take them all on the same date; either way you must complete all three sections in order to pass the exam. While you may also be required to take other tests developed or approved by the California Commission on Teacher Credentialing (CTC) for specific academic subjects, the core subjects tested on the CBEST are essential for anyone entering the teaching profession.

WHAT'S ON THE CBEST?

The CBEST gauges college-level mathematics, reading, and writing skills. Each section—Mathematics, Reading, and Writing—is broken down into different categories based on the skills needed to succeed in a teacher preparation program.

The Mathematics section focuses on estimation, measurement, statistical principles, problem solving, computation, and numerical and graphic relationships. You may not use a calculator.

On the Reading section, you will read and answer questions concerning passages about varying topics. Expect to analyze tables and graphs as well. The section addresses critical analysis and evaluation, and research and comprehension. Questions test your critical thinking, analytical, and research skills as well as reading comprehension.

On the Writing section, you must write two essays responding to two topics. In one, you will be provided with a specific statement or situation, which you must analyze. In the other essay, you will be asked to discuss a personal experience. The Writing section measures your language and compositional skills.

You are always allotted four hours for the CBEST whether you take one, two, or all three sections. You may choose which sections to take and how many; regardless of your choices, you will have four hours during which you will divide and manage your time. This time period includes fifteen minutes to complete a nondisclosure agreement and tutorial.

What's on the California Basic Educational Skills Test (CBEST)?

Section	Concepts	Number of Questions	Time
Mathematics	Estimation, measurement, and statistical principles; computation and problem solving; and numerical and graphical relationships	50 multiple-choice questions	
Reading	Critical analysis and evaluation; comprehension and research skills	50 multiple-choice questions	
Writing	Purpose, audience, text structure, argument or claim, supporting details, language skills	2 essays	

Section	Concepts	Number of Questions	Time
Total		100 multiple-choice questions and 2 essays	4 hours (allotted for test time regardless of number of sections you take)

How is the CBEST Scored?

Your preliminary scores for the Reading and Mathematics sections are immediately available upon completion. Official scores are released up to two weeks after taking the test. It can take up to an additional two weeks to receive your Writing scores. Once your scores are posted, they will only remain available for sixty days. Your CBEST scores will automatically be sent to the California Department of Education's Bureau of Educator Certification; however to have them sent to a college or university, you must make a request when you register for the exam.

Each multiple-choice question is worth one raw point. The total number of questions you answer correctly is added up to obtain your raw score. Your raw score is then scaled; a minimum scaled score of 123 is required to pass the CBEST. Scaled scores for individual sections range from 20 to 80. A scaled score of 41 is required to pass individual sections of the test; however, you may pass the whole CBEST with a scaled score of 37 on one or two sections if your total score is 123 or more. If any section is *below* 37, though, you will not pass.

Keep in mind that a small number of multiple-choice questions are experimental and will not count toward your overall score. ETS uses these to test out new questions for future exams. However, as those questions are not indicated on the test, you must respond to every question.

There is no penalty for guessing on the CBEST, so be sure to eliminate answer choices and answer every question. If you still do not know the answer, guess; you may get it right!

How is the CBEST Administered?

The CBEST is both computer- and paper-based. The computer-based test is offered continuously at a range of universities and testing centers. The paper-based test is offered approximately every three months. It may be taken in its individual parts or all at once. Check http://ctcexams.nesinc.com for more information. You will need to print your registration ticket from your online account and bring it, along with your identification, to the testing site on test day. No pens, pencils, erasers, or calculators are allowed. If you are taking the computer-based test, you will be provided with a pen and scratch paper to take notes or prepare your responses to the Writing section.

About Cirrus Test Prep

Cirrus Test Prep study guides are designed by current and former educators and are tailored to meet your needs as an incoming educator. Our guides offer all of the resources necessary to help you pass teacher certification tests across the nation.

Cirrus clouds are graceful, wispy clouds characterized by their high altitude. Just like cirrus clouds, Cirrus Test Prep's goal is to help educators "aim high" when it comes to obtaining their teacher certification and entering the classroom.

About This Guide

This guide will help you master the most important test topics and also develop critical test-taking skills. We have built features into our books to prepare you for your tests and increase your score. Along with a detailed summary of the test's format, content, and scoring, we offer an in-depth overview of the content knowledge required to pass the test. Our sidebars provide interesting information, highlight key concepts, and review content so that you can solidify your understanding of the exam's concepts. Test your knowledge with sample questions and detailed answer explanations in the text that help you think through the problems on the exam, and with two full-length practice tests that reflect the content and format of the CBEST. We're pleased you've chosen Cirrus to be a part of your professional journey!

Reading

When the Spanish-American War broke out in 1898, the officer corps was composed of veterans of the Civil War and the Indian Wars. With more volunteers than it could accept, the army set high standards: all the recruits had to be skilled on horseback and with guns. Consequently, they became known as the Rough Riders.

From the passage, it can be inferred that recruits needed to be "skilled on horseback" for what reason?

Between November 15 and December 21, 1864, Major General William Tecumseh Sherman marched Union troops from the recently captured city of Atlanta to the port of Savannah. The goal was not only to capture the port city and secure Georgia for the Union, but also to destroy the Confederacy's infrastructure and demoralize its people.

Where did General Sherman and his troops begin marching on November 15?

The recruits probably needed to be skilled on horseback because the soldiers would be cavalry or mounted troops.

Atlanta, Georgia; the text says that they marched "from the recently captured city of Atlanta to the port of Savannah."

Activity level has a significant impact on a patient's energy needs. A bedridden patient will obviously expend fewer calories and thus will need to eat fewer. An elderly, bedridden women can need as little as 8.5 calories per pound of body weight: if such a patient weighed 135 pounds, she would need only 1150 calories a day.

What causes a bedridden patient to need fewer calories per day than she would need if she were not bedridden?

In 1864, marching from Atlanta to Savannah, General Sherman and his Union troops destroyed rail lines and burned buildings and fields. They packed only twenty days' worth of rations, foraging for the rest of their supplies from farms along the way. By the time they reached Savannah, they had destroyed 300 miles of railroad, countless cotton gins and mills, seized 4,000 mules, 13,000 head of cattle, 9.5 million pounds of corn, and 10.5 million pounds of fodder. Sherman estimated his troops inflicted $100 million in damages.

What did the Union troops do after using up the rations they packed?

The Battle of Little Bighorn, commonly called Custer's Last Stand, was a battle between the Lakota, the Northern Cheyenne, the Arapaho, and the Seventh Calvary Regiment of the US Army. Led by war leaders Crazy Horse and Chief Gall and the religious leader Sitting Bull, the allied tribes of the Plains Indians decisively defeated their U.S. foes. Two hundred and sixty-eight U.S. soldiers were killed, including General George Armstrong Custer, two of his brothers, his nephew, his brother-in-law, and six Indian scouts.

What is this passage's main idea?

Someone who stays in bed all the time is less active than someone who is not bedridden. The less active someone is, the fewer calories she needs.

They used supplies that they "foraged" (took or stole) "from farms along the way." These supplies included cattle, corn, and fodder.

"The allied tribes of the Plains Indians decisively defeated their U.S. foes." All the details in the passage support this main idea.

The Gatling gun, a forerunner of the modern machine gun, was an early rapid-fire spring loaded, hand-cranked weapon. In 1861, Dr. Richard J. Gatling designed the gun to allow one person to fire many shots quickly. His goal was to reduce the death toll of war by decreasing the number of soldiers needed to fight.

Did Dr. Gatling's gun probably "reduce the death toll of war"? Why or why not?

In December of 1944, Germany launched its last major offensive campaign of World War II, pushing through the dense forests of the Ardennes region of Belgium, France, and Luxembourg. Due to troop positioning, the Americans bore the brunt of the attack, incurring 100,000 deaths, the highest number of casualties of any battle during the war. However, after a month of grueling fighting in the bitter cold, a lack of fuel and a masterful American military strategy resulted in an Allied victory that sealed Germany's fate.

How did a lack of fuel "result in an Allied victory"?

The cisco, a foot-long freshwater fish native to the Great Lakes, had almost died out by the 1950s, but today it thrives. The cisco have an invasive species, quagga mussels, to thank for their return. Quagga mussels depleted nutrients in the lakes, harming other species highly dependent on these nutrients. Cisco, however, thrive in low-nutrient environments. As other species—many invasive— diminished, cisco flourished in their place.

How did quagga mussels prevent the cisco's extinction?

No, probably not: his gun could kill more enemy soldiers in a shorter time. Also, its invention led to the creation of the "modern machine gun," which could kill an even greater number of people in an even shorter time.

The Germans lacked fuel and so could not move their troops and equipment around efficiently. This and "a masterful American military strategy" allowed the Allies to win.

Quagga mussels depleted nutrients in the Great Lakes, harming species that needed them. Since the cisco thrives in low-nutrient environments, and because it now had fewer species to compete with, this freshwater fish stopped dying out and began to thrive again.

In 1953, doctors surgically removed the hippocampus of patient Henry Molaison in an attempt to stop his frequent seizures. Unexpectedly, he lost the ability to form new memories, leading to the biggest breakthrough in the science of memory. Molaison's long-term memory—of events more than a year before his surgery—was unchanged as was his ability to learn physical skills. From this, scientists learned that different types of memory are handled by different parts of the brain.

Based on the text, which part of the brain probably handles the task of forming new memories?

In the 1950s, scientists learned that different types of memory are handled by different parts of the brain, with the hippocampus responsible for *episodic memory*, the short-term recall of events. Researchers have since discovered that some memories are then channeled to the cortex, the outer layers of the brain that handle higher functions, where they are gradually integrated with related information to build lasting knowledge about our world.

Where is the brain's cortex located?

Researchers at the University of California, Berkeley, decided to tackle an age-old problem: why shoelaces come untied. They recorded the shoelaces of a volunteer walking on a treadmill by attaching devices to record the acceleration, or g-force, experienced by the knot. The results were surprising. A shoelace knot experiences more g-force from a person walking than any rollercoaster can generate.

What is this passage mainly about?

The hippocampus probably handles the task of forming new memories—after doctors removed Molaison's hippocampus, "he lost the ability to form new memories."

The cortex is the brain's "outer layers."

The passage is mainly about researchers who tried to figure out why shoelaces come untied. All the details in the passage support this main idea.

In recent years, hand sanitizers have become popular as an alternative to hand washing. These gels, liquids, and foams contain a high concentration of alcohol (usually at least 60 percent) that kills most bacteria and fungi; they can also be effective against some, but not all, viruses. There is a downside to hand sanitizer, however. Because the sanitizer isn't rinsed from hands, it only kills pathogens and does nothing to remove organic matter. So, hands "cleaned" with hand sanitizer may still harbor pathogens.

In what important way is handwashing more effective than using hand sanitizer?

Archaeologists have discovered the oldest known specimens of bedbugs in a cave in Oregon where humans once lived. The three different species date back to between 5,000 and 11,000 years ago. The finding gives scientists a clue as to how bedbugs became human parasites. These bedbugs, like those that plague humans today, originated as bat parasites. Scientists hypothesize that it was the co-habitation of humans and bats in the caves that encouraged the bugs to begin feeding on the humans.

What happened after humans began sleeping in caves where bats lived?

Archaeologists have discovered the oldest known specimens of bedbugs in a cave in Oregon where humans once lived. The three species found in the Oregon caves are actually still around today, although they continue to prefer bats. Humans only lived seasonally in the Oregon cave system, however, which might explain why these insects did not fully transfer to human hosts like bedbugs elsewhere did.

Today, why do the three species of bedbugs "continue to prefer bats" to humans?

Handwashing rinses away organic matter that may contain pathogens; since sanitizer is not rinsed from the hands, it may leave organic matter behind.

After humans began sleeping in caves, species that originated as bat parasites became human parasites as well. Eventually, humans named such parasites "bedbugs."

The bedbugs probably did not "fully transfer to human hosts" because humans did not live year-round in the caves where the bedbugs lived.

The Bastille, Paris's famous historical prison, was originally built in 1370 as a fortification, called a *bastide* in Old French, to protect the city from English invasion during the Hundred Years' War. It rose 100 feet into the air, had eight towers, and was surrounded by a moat more than eighty feet wide.

Use context to define the word *fortification* in this passage.

At midnight on Saturday, August 12, 1961, units of the East German army moved into position and began closing the border between East and West Berlin. Destroying streets that ran parallel to the border to make them impassable, they installed ninety-seven miles of barbed wire and fences around West Berlin and another twenty-seven miles along the border between West and East Berlin.

Was the author's main purpose for writing this passage to inform readers or to express an opinion?

In Zimbardo's famous prison experiment, the participants, all healthy, stable, intelligent male Stanford University students, were classified as either guards or prisoners and told they would be acting their parts in a simulated prison environment.... Even giving individuals temporary power over others was enough to completely alter the way they viewed and behaved toward each other. Indeed, the behaviors Zimbardo witnessed in each of the groups were not a result of the dispositions of the participants but of the situation in which they had been placed.

What caused the participants' "behavior toward each other" to "completely alter"?

The passage says that the Bastille was originally a fortification meant "to protect [Paris] from English invasion," so a fortification must be a fort—a protective structure meant to keep enemies out.

The author's main purpose is to inform readers; no opinions are expressed, only facts.

The situation they were in (acting the parts of prison guards and prisoners in a "simulated prison environment") caused the participants' behavior to change.

By Sunday morning, August 13, 1961, the border between East and West Berlin was completely shut down. Families woke up that morning suddenly divided, and some East Berliners with jobs in the west were unable to get to work. West Berlin was now an isolated island surrounded by a communist government hostile to its existence.

How can you tell from this passage that the border was shut down very quickly?

In 1989, almost a million Chinese university students descended on central Beijing, protesting for increased democracy and calling for the resignation of Communist Party leaders. For three weeks, they marched, chanted, and held daily vigils in the city's Tiananmen Square. The protests had widespread support in China, particularly among factory workers who cheered them on. For Westerners watching, it seemed to be the beginning of a political revolution in China.

When and where did the student protests occur?

One of the most dramatic acts of nonviolent resistance in India's movement for independence from Britain came in 1930, when independence leader Mahatma Gandhi organized a 240-mile march to the Arabian Sea. The goal of the march was to make salt from seawater, in defiance of British law. The British prohibited Indians from collecting or selling salt—a vital part of the Indian diet—requiring them instead to buy it from British merchants and pay a heavy salt tax.

Why didn't British authorities want the Indians to make, collect, or sell salt?

The phrase "woke up that morning suddenly divided" implies that this event occurred overnight.

In 1989, in Tiananmen Square in central Beijing, China.

Probably because the British wanted the money they earned from selling and taxing salt; also, this may have been a way for the British to exert control over the Indian people.

The Scream of Nature by Edvard Munch has four different versions: two paintings and two pastels. The Munch Museum in Oslo holds a painted version and a pastel version, while the National Gallery in Oslo holds the other painting. In 1994 the National Gallery's version was stolen, and in 2004 the painting at the Munch Museum was stolen at gunpoint in the middle of the day. Both paintings were eventually recovered. In 2012, the second pastel version was sold at auction for almost $120 million.

How many versions of the artwork were stolen, and how many versions were sold?

After World War I, some American writers, raised on the values of the prewar world, felt frustrated with what they viewed as the superficiality and materialism of postwar American culture. Many of them, like Ernest Hemingway and F. Scott Fitzgerald, fled to Paris, where they became known as the "lost generation," creating a trove of literary works criticizing their home culture and delving into their own feelings of alienation.

Use context to define the word *trove* in this passage.

The American love affair with popcorn began in 1912, when popcorn was first sold in theaters. The popcorn industry flourished during the Great Depression when it was advertised as a wholesome and economical food. Selling for five to ten cents a bag, it was a luxury that the downtrodden could afford. With the introduction of mobile popcorn machines at the World's Columbian Exposition, popcorn moved from the theater into fairs and parks.

Use context to define the word *downtrodden*.

Two versions, both paintings, were stolen and have been recovered. One version, a pastel, sold at auction in 2012 for almost $120 million.

A treasure trove is a collection of valuable metals, coins, and jewels, so a "trove of literary works" must be a collection of valuable literary works: a trove must be a collection of valuable items.

During the Great Depression, many people lost their jobs, so they were very poor. By "the downtrodden," the author must mean poor people, people who were beaten down—demoralized—by hard economic times.

I stand before you tonight under indictment for the alleged crime of having voted at the last presidential election, without having a lawful right to vote. It shall be my work this evening to prove to you that in thus voting, I not only committed no crime, but, instead, simply exercised my citizen's rights, guaranteed to me and all United States citizens by the National Constitution, beyond the power of any state to deny.

What is Anthony's main argument in this passage?

In an effort to increase women's presence in government, several countries in Latin America, including Argentina, Brazil, and Mexico, have implemented legislated candidate quotas. These quotas require that at least 30 percent of a party's candidate list in any election cycle consists of women who have a legitimate chance at election. As a result, Latin America has the greatest number of female heads of government in the world, and the second highest percentage of female members of parliament after Nordic Europe.

Why does Latin America have "the greatest number of female heads of government in the world"?

Tourists flock to Yellowstone National Park each year to view the geysers that bubble and erupt throughout it. What most of these tourists do not know is that these geysers are formed by a caldera, a hot crater in the earth's crust, that was created by a series of three eruptions of an ancient supervolcano. These eruptions, which began 2.1 million years ago, spewed between 1,000 to 2,450 cubic kilometers of volcanic matter at such a rate that the volcano's magma chamber collapsed, creating the craters.

What resulted from an ancient supervolcano's three eruptions?

She argues that women have the right to vote in the United States because the Constitution says they do.

Because several Latin American countries have "implemented legislated candidate quotas . . . [that] require that at least 30 percent of a party's candidate list in any election cycle [to consist] of women who have a legitimate chance at election."

The three eruptions caused the volcano's magma chamber to collapse. Then a "caldera, a hot crater in the earth's crust" formed in the area where Yellowstone National Park is located today. The caldera formed "geysers that bubble and erupt."

Increasingly, companies are turning to subcontracting services rather than hiring full-time employees. Recently, the courts have grappled with questions about the hiring company's responsibility in maintaining fair labor practices. Companies argue that they delegate that authority to the subcontractors, while unions and other worker advocate groups argue that companies still have a legal obligation to the workers who contribute to their business.

Why might companies prefer using subcontracting services to hiring full-time employees?

In 1974, scientists uncovered in Africa's Rift Valley a 3.2 million-year-old non-human hominid they nicknamed "Lucy." And, in 2013, researchers found the oldest fossil in the human ancestral line. Before this, the oldest fossil from the genus *Homo*—of which *Homo sapiens* are the only remaining species—dated only back to 2.3 million years ago, leaving a 700,000 gap between Lucy's species and the advent of humans. The new fossil dated back to 2.75 and 2.8 million years ago, pushing the appearance of humans back 400,000 years.

Name two important differences between "Lucy" and the fossil discovered in 2013.

There are many situations when measuring temperature orally isn't an option. Some people, like agitated patients or fussy babies, won't be able to sit still long enough for an accurate reading. In these situations, it's best to use a thermometer that works much more quickly, such as one that measures temperature in the ear or at the temporal artery.

In what situation is it "best to use a thermometer that works much more quickly, such as one that measures temperature in the ear or at the temporal artery"?

It is probably cheaper to use subcontracting services. For full-time employees, businesses must pay for benefits such as sick days and health care.

"Lucy" was a "non-human hominid," and the fossil discovered in 2013 was "in the human ancestral line." "Lucy" was 3.2 million years old, and the 2013 fossil was about 2.8 million years old—so "Lucy" was about 400,000 years older.

When a patient cannot "sit still long enough for an accurate reading"; two examples of such a patient are an agitated person or a fussy baby.

A study of people who'd lost a high percentage of their body weight (>17%) in a short period of time found that they could not physically maintain their new weight. Scientists measured their resting metabolic rate and found that they'd need to consume only a few hundred calories a day to meet their metabolic needs. Basically, their bodies were in starvation mode and seemed to desperately hang on to each and every calorie.

Why did dieters' bodies go into "starvation mode"?

In recent decades, jazz has been associated with New Orleans and festivals like Mardi Gras, but in the 1920s, jazz was a booming trend whose influence reached into many aspects of American culture. In fact, the years between World War I and the Great Depression were known as the Jazz Age, a term coined by F. Scott Fitzgerald in his famous novel *The Great Gatsby*. Sometimes also called the Roaring Twenties, this period saw major urban centers experiencing new economic, cultural, and artistic vitality.

Who first called the 1920s "the Jazz Age"?

During the 1920s in the United States, musicians flocked to cities such as New York and Chicago, which would become famous hubs for jazz musicians. Ella Fitzgerald, for example, moved from Virginia to New York City to begin her much-lauded singing career, and jazz pioneer Louis Armstrong got his big break in Chicago.

What did Ella Fitzgerald and Louis Armstrong have in common?

Dieters' bodies went into "starvation mode" because they had "lost a high percentage of their body weight (>17%) in a short period of time." Apparently, when someone loses a lot of weight in a short period of time, the body "thinks" it is starving and "desperately [hangs] on to each and every calorie."

Writer F. Scott Fitzgerald coined this term in his novel *The Great Gatsby.*

Both were 1920s jazz musicians who became famous when performing in big U.S. cities such as New York and Chicago.

The most important part of brewing coffee is using the right water. Choose a water that you think has a nice, neutral flavor. Anything with too many minerals or contaminants will change the flavor of the coffee, and water with too few minerals won't do a good job of extracting the flavor from the coffee beans. Water should be heated to between 195 and 205 degrees Fahrenheit. Boiling water (212 degrees Fahrenheit) will burn the beans and give your coffee a scorched flavor.

What is the author's main purpose for writing this passage? How can you tell?

While the water is heating, grind your coffee beans. Remember, the fresher the grind, the fresher the flavor of the coffee. The number of beans is entirely dependent on your personal taste. Obviously, more beans will result in a more robust flavor, while fewer beans will give your coffee a more subtle taste. The texture of the grind should be not too fine (which can lead to bitter coffee) or too large (which can lead to weak coffee).

Why do you think too-large coffee grounds can "lead to weak coffee"?

Once your coffee beans are ground and the water has reached the perfect temperature, you're ready to brew. A French press (which we recommend), allows you to control brewing time and provide a thorough brew. Pour the grounds into the press, then pour the hot water over the grounds and let it steep. The brew shouldn't require more than 5 minutes, although those of you who like your coffee a bit harsher can leave it longer. Finally, use the plunger to remove the grounds and pour.

What should you do after "pour[ing] the grounds into the press"?

The author's main purpose is to teach readers how to make good coffee. The author furnishes detailed instructions to produce a good result.

Large (coarse) coffee grounds probably do not produce strong coffee because the hot water does not have enough access to coarse-ground coffee beans' surfaces.

After "pour[ing] the grounds into the press," you should "pour the hot water over the grounds and let it steep."

According to Martin Seligman's 2011 book *Flourish: A Visionary New Understanding of Happiness and Well-being*, positive psychology began as an inquiry into the experiences that contribute to life satisfaction. Through his theory of authentic happiness, Seligman posited that human happiness could be understood in terms of three elements, all of which we pursue for their inherent value—positive emotions (like joy, amusement, and gratitude), engagement (the tendency to lose oneself in activity), and meaning (the extent to which one believes his or her life has purpose).

Seligman's "three elements" are engagement, meaning, and what?

Influenza (also called the flu) has historically been one of the most common, and deadliest, human infections. While many people who contract the virus will recover, many others will not. Over the past 150 years, tens of millions of people have died from the flu, and millions more have been left with lingering complications such as secondary infections.

Which sentence expresses this passage's main idea?

Although it's a common disease, the flu is not actually highly infectious, meaning it's relatively difficult to contract. The flu can only be transmitted when individuals come into direct contact with bodily fluids of people infected with the flu or when they are exposed to expelled aerosol particles (which result from coughing and sneezing).

Which would be more likely to give you the flu: shaking hands with an infected person or sharing a drinking glass with that person?

The third element is "positive emotions (like joy, amusement, and gratitude)."

The first sentence expresses the main idea: "Influenza (also called the flu) has historically been one of the most common, and deadliest, human infections."

Sharing a drinking glass with an infected person would be more likely to give you the flu. Sharing a glass would probably cause you to "come into direct contact with" the infected person's saliva, a "bodily fluid." (If the person had just sneezed or coughed into her hands, shaking hands with her could give you the flu, too, but then you would have to lick your fingers to transmit the virus to your body.)

One of the reasons the flu has historically been so deadly is the amount of time between when people become infectious and when they develop symptoms. Viral shedding—the process by which the body releases viruses that have been successfully reproducing during the infection—takes place two days after infection, while symptoms do not usually develop until the third day of infection. Thus, infected individuals have at least twenty-four hours in which they may unknowingly infect others.

What happens after infection occurs but before flu symptoms develop?

A fault of disproportionate height of ceilings must be avoided when renovating a house. A ten-foot room with a thirteen-foot ceiling makes the narrowness of the room doubly apparent; one feels shut up between two walls which threaten to come together and squeeze one between them, while, on the other hand, a ten-foot room with a nine-foot ceiling may have a really comfortable and cozy effect.

Why does the author believe that "a ten-foot room with a thirteen-foot ceiling makes the narrowness of the room doubly apparent"?

It seemed to Julia as if the other drivers on the road felt as sluggish and surly as as she did—it took her an extra fifteen minutes to get to work. And when she arrived, all the parking spots were full. By the time she'd finally found a spot in the overflow lot, she was thirty minutes late for work. She'd hoped her boss would be too busy to notice, but he'd already put a pile of paperwork on her desk with a note that simply said "Rewrite."

How does Julia know that her boss *has* noticed that she is late for work?

Viral shedding occurs two days after infection and one day before flu symptoms develop.

The author thinks that a smallish room with a too-high ceiling "makes the narrowness of the room doubly apparent; one feels shut up between two walls which threaten to come together and squeeze one between them."

He has already put a pile of paperwork on her desk, so he must have noticed that she was not there on time.

Today, social psychologists study the effect of social influence on a number of different behaviors: conformity, obedience, aggression, prejudice, and even attraction and love. The insights these researchers have gained have laid the foundation for further examination of human social behavior and, ultimately, for a refined approach to legal and social policy.

How might "social influence" affect an individual's "prejudice"?

William James, 1842–1910, explained, "you must simply work your pupil into such a state of interest in what you are going to teach him that every other object of attention is banished from his mind; then reveal it to him so impressively that he will remember the occasion to his dying day; and finally fill him with devouring curiosity to know what the next steps in connection with the subject are." Within these practical guidelines, a teacher must apply creativity, awareness of student knowledge, and perception of student interests and needs.

What does James mean by "devouring curiosity"?

The bacteria, fungi, insects, plants, and animals that live together in a habitat have evolved to share a pool of limited resources. They've competed for water, minerals, nutrients, sunlight, and space—sometimes for thousands or even millions of years. As these communities have evolved, the species in them have developed complex, long-term interspecies interactions known as symbiotic relationships.

What is a "symbiotic relationship"? Use context to help you define this term.

If someone's family, friends, teachers, and other influential people hold certain prejudices, it is likely that person will grow up holding the same prejudices.

He means curiosity so strong that it "devours" all or most other concerns—the person *has* to know the answer as soon as possible.

A symbiotic relationship between two species is a "complex, long-term interspecies interaction."

Examples of symbiotic relationships (long-term interspecies interactions) can easily be seen in any ecosystem. In mutualism, both individuals benefit. Pollination, for example, is mutualistic—pollinators get nutrients from the flower, and the plant is able to reproduce. A relationship where one individual benefits and the other is harmed is known as parasitism. Tapeworms, which steal nutrients from their host, are parasitic.

Use context to define the term *parasitism*. Give an example of this kind of relationship.

Commensalism is a relationship where one species benefits and the other is unaffected. Remoras, for instance, will attach themselves to sharks and eat the food particles they leave behind. It might seem like the shark gets nothing from the relationship, but a closer look will show that sharks in fact benefit from remoras, which clean the sharks' skin and remove parasites.

Is the relationship between sharks and remoras a good example of commensalism? Why or why not?

Hand washing is one of our simplest and most powerful weapons against infection. The idea behind hand washing is deceptively simple. Many illnesses are spread when people touch infected surfaces, such as door handles or other people's hands, and then touch their own eyes, mouths, or noses. So, if pathogens can be removed from the hands before they spread, infections can be prevented.

How does frequent handwashing lessen the chance that people will transfer pathogens to their own eyes, mouths, or noses?

Parasitism is a symbiotic relationship in which "one individual benefits and the other is harmed." For example, a tapeworm benefits from its relationship with its host, but the host suffers (since the worm "steals" a portion of the host's nutrients).

No, neither of the species is "unaffected" by the relationship. Both species benefit from it.

When people touch surfaces such as door handles, they can pick up pathogens that others have left there. However, handwashing can remove pathogens before a person touches his own eyes, mouth, or nose. In this case, he will not become infected.

In 2014, researchers of veterinary medicine at the University of Perugia in Italy completed a review of the diagnostic tools and strategies available to today's practitioners and found a number of them to be effective. Presumptive diagnosis, the first of these strategies, involves making a prediction about the animal's pain based on the observable damage to the body or body part. As with human pain, greater damage or disfigurement likely suggests more significant pain.

Where and when did veterinary researchers "[complete] a review of the diagnostic tools and strategies available to today's practitioners"?

...it is a downright mockery to talk to women of their enjoyment of the blessings of liberty while they are denied the use of the only means of securing them provided by this democratic-republican government—the ballot.

For any state to make sex a qualification that must ever result in the disfranchisement of one entire half of the people, is...a violation of the supreme law of the land. By it the blessings of liberty are forever withheld from women and their female posterity.

What is Anthony's main point about "the blessings of liberty"?

William James, 1842–1910, was an influential American philosopher and psychologist who studied the human psyche. James stated, "A science only lays down lines within which the rules of the art must fall, laws which the follower of the art must not transgress; but what particular thing he shall positively do within those lines is left exclusively to his own genius. One genius will do his work well and succeed in one way, while another succeeds as well quite differently; yet neither will transgress the lines."

Use context to figure out what the word *transgress* means in this passage.

In 2014 at the University of Perugia in Italy.

She argues that unless U.S. women gain the right to vote, they will never really be free, as the Constitution says they should be.

In this passage, the word *transgress* means "to cross boundaries (rules) within which one is supposed to stay."

When done correctly, hand washing can prevent the spread of many dangerous bacteria and viruses, including those that cause the flu, the common cold, diarrhea, and many acute respiratory illnesses. The most basic method of hand washing involves only soap and water. Just twenty seconds of scrubbing with soap and a complete rinsing with water is enough to kill and/or wash away many pathogens. The process doesn't even require warm water.

Can you kill or wash away pathogens with soap and cool water?

The energy needs of patients can vary widely. Generally, energy needs are directly related to a person's weight and inversely related to age; it's also generally true that men require more calories than women. Thus, a thirty-five-year-old woman who weighs 135 pounds will require around 1800 calories a day, while an older woman would require fewer, and a heavier woman would require more. A man of the same age and weight would require 2000 calories a day.

If a sixty-year-old woman who weighs 135 pounds eats 1,800 or more calories a day, what will probably happen?

During the 1920s in the United States, jazz music was played by and for a more expressive and freed populace than the United States had previously seen. Women gained the right to vote and were openly seen drinking and dancing to jazz music. This period marked the emergence of the flapper, a woman determined to make a statement about her new role in society.

How was "the flapper" different from earlier generations of women in the United States?

Yes, as long as you scrub for at least twenty seconds.

She will probably gain weight. The passage says that "an older woman [who weighs 135 pounds] would require fewer [calories per day than 1,800]."

Unlike earlier generations of U.S. women, flappers had the right to vote. They drank alcoholic beverages, danced to jazz music, and made "statement[s] about [their] new role in society."

Food historians believe that popcorn is one of the earliest uses of cultivated corn. In 1948, Herbert Dick and Earle Smith discovered old popcorn dating back 4000 years in the New Mexico Bat Cave. For the Aztec Indians who called the caves home, popcorn (or *momochitl*) played an important role in society, both as a food staple and in ceremonies. The Aztecs cooked popcorn by heating sand in a fire; when it was heated, kernels were added and would pop when exposed to the heat of the sand.

What did the Aztecs do after heating sand in a fire?

Credit scores, which range from 300 to 850, are a single value that summarizes an individual's credit history. Pay your bills late? Your credit score will be lower than someone who gets that electric bill filed on the first of every month. Just paid off your massive student loans? You can expect your credit score to shoot up. The companies that compile credit scores actually keep track of all the loans, credit cards, and bill payments in your name.

What is the highest possible credit score?

On November 20, 1969, about 90 people from an activist group, Indians of All Tribes, sailed to Alcatraz Island in San Francisco Bay, claiming it for all the tribes of North America. Their demands were ignored, so the group continued to occupy the island for the next 19 months, its numbers swelling up to 600 as others joined. By January of 1970, many of the original protestors had left, and on June 11, 1971 federal marshals forcibly removed the last residents.

When did the occupation begin and end, and how long did it last?

They added corn kernels to the heated sand; this caused the kernels to pop, forming popcorn.

The highest possible credit score is 850; the passage says that "credit scores . . . range from 300 to 850."

It began on November 20, 1969, and ended on June 11, 1971; it lasted for about nineteen months.

Having no credit score can often be just as bad as having a low one. Lenders want to know that you have a history of borrowing money and paying it back on time. After all, if you've never taken out a loan, how can a bank know that you'll pay back its money? So, having nothing on your credit report can result in low credit limits and high interest rates.

What is this passage's main idea?

Every morning now brought its regular duties—shops were to be visited; some new part of the town to be looked at; and the pump-room to be attended, where they paraded up and down for an hour, looking at everybody and speaking to no one. The wish of a numerous acquaintance in Bath was still uppermost with Mrs. Allen, and she repeated it after every fresh proof, which every morning brought, of her knowing nobody at all.

Where does this part of the novel take place?

In his treatise *Politics*, Aristotle wrote, "Man is by nature a social animal; an individual who is unsocial naturally and not accidentally is either beneath our notice or more than human. Society is something in nature that precedes the individual. Anyone who either cannot lead the common life or is so self-sufficient as not to need to, and therefore does not partake of society, is either a beast or a god."

What are two probable reasons why Aristotle wrote this section of his treatise *Politics*?

The main idea is expressed in the first sentence: "Having no credit score can often be just as bad as having a low one." The other sentences in the passage tell more about this main idea.

In a town called Bath; Mrs. Allen is apparently on a visit to Bath and wishes to get to know new people there; however, so far she has become acquainted with "nobody at all."

One reason is to inform readers about individuals' relationship to society, and another is to express his opinions about this topic.

Social psychologists have been studying the effect of societal influences on human behavior for decades, and a number of fascinating findings have been the result. Together, these discoveries have shed light on one clear truth—that human behavior cannot be understood in a vacuum; that is, our daily behaviors are inextricably linked with the social context in which they occur.

What evidence does the author give to support the argument that "human behavior cannot be understood in a vacuum"?

In 1989, almost a million Chinese university students descended on central Beijing, protesting for increased democracy. The world was stunned when, on July 4, Chinese troops and security police stormed the square, firing into the crowd. Chaos erupted with some students trying to fight back by throwing stones and setting fire to military vehicles. Tens of thousands more attempted to flee. While official numbers were never given, observers estimated anywhere from 300 to thousands of people were killed, while 10,000 were arrested.

It can be inferred from the passage that Chinese authorities killed and arrested student protesters for what reason?

If you have ever been cut off in the middle of bad city traffic, you may have immediately assumed that the offender was inconsiderate or incompetent. While this may be true, it may be equally likely that the person is dealing with an emergency situation or that they simply did not see you. According to psychologist Eliot Aronson, this tendency to attribute behaviors, especially negative behaviors, to disposition is risky and can ultimately be detrimental to us and to the other person.

What does *detrimental* mean in this passage? How do you know?

The author says that social psychologists have made "fascinating findings" that "shed light on" the premise that "our daily behaviors are inextricably linked with the social context in which they occur."

They probably killed and arrested the protesters to assert their authority and to quash demands for increased democracy; clearly, the existing Chinese government leaders did not want a more democratic government.

It means "damaging." The author is saying that if we assume someone who cuts us off in traffic is an "inconsiderate or incompetent" person, we may be overlooking an explanation that does not support such assumptions. This could be "detrimental" to us and to the other person if, for example, we get angry and cause a car accident.

At the beginning of Philip Zimbardo's famous prison experiment, the participants, all healthy, stable, intelligent male Stanford University students, were classified as either guards or prisoners and told they would be acting their parts in a simulated prison environment for two weeks. However, after just six days, Zimbardo had to terminate the experiment because of the extreme behaviors he was witnessing in both groups: prisoners had become entirely submissive to and resentful of the guards, while the guards had become cruel and unrelenting in their treatment of the prisoners.

How did the experiment cause participants to act?

In the early twenty-first century, a new perspective on psychology emerged when Dr. Martin E. P. Seligman received funding to begin research into an idea that he referred to as positive psychology, a field that would be concerned with understanding the factors that contribute not to psychological distress but to an individual's ability to live a happy, fulfilling, productive life.

How was Dr. Seligman's "positive psychology" approach different from earlier methods of treating patients?

Concerns about animal suffering have led to major changes in a variety of industries from entertainment to food production. In the field of veterinary medicine, this new line of inquiry—into whether animals experience pain and suffering the same way humans do—is especially clear when explored in the context of pain management.

What types of "major changes" might "concern about animal suffering" have led people to make in the "food production" industry?

The ones playing prisoners became "entirely submissive to and resentful of the guards," while the ones playing guards became "cruel and unrelenting in their treatment of the prisoners."

Instead of focusing on "understanding the factors that contribute . . . to psychological distress," Seligman's approach focused on "an individual's ability to live a happy, fulfilling, productive life."

Maybe the industry has made greater efforts to make sure that animals like chickens, pigs, and cows have more comfortable lives before they are slaughtered for food. Maybe the industry has tried to make methods of slaughtering animals more humane.

In general, you can take a number of basic steps to raise your credit score. First, ensure that payments are made on time. When payments are past due, it not only has a negative impact on your score, but new creditors will be reluctant to lend while you are delinquent on other accounts. Being smart about taking on debt is another key factor in keeping your credit score high.

Which phrase in the passage has the same meaning as the word *delinquent*?

One myth that prevents the advancement of pain management practices is the myth that pain is a necessary part of an animal's recovery. While some veterinarians believe that pain may prevent a healing dog, for example, from playing too vigorously, Dr. Debbie Grant says this is simply not the case. In fact, restlessness and discomfort may even lead to unusually high levels of agitation and may consequently slow the recovery process even further.

Regarding the idea that "pain is a necessary part of an animal's recovery," how does Dr. Grant's opinion differ from those of "some [other] veterinarians?

I slept sounder than ever I remembered to have done in my life, and, as I reckoned, about nine hours; for, when I awaked, it was just daylight. I attempted to rise, but was not able to stir: for as I happened to lie on my back, I found my arms and legs were strongly fastened on each side to the ground; and my hair, which was long and thick, tied down in the same manner. I likewise felt several slender ligatures across my body, from my arm-pits to my thighs.

What has happened to the narrator?

The phrase "past due" has the same meaning as *delinquent.*

Dr. Grant thinks that this is a myth, and that "restlessness and discomfort may even lead to unusually high levels of agitation and may consequently slow the recovery process even further." The other vets "believe that pain may prevent a healing dog, for example, from playing too vigorously."

While he was sleeping very soundly, one or more people have apparently tied him with "ligatures," fastening his whole body to the ground.

Veterinarians have a unique challenge when it comes to diagnosing their patients. Unlike doctors, who typically have the benefit of discussing their patients' concerns, veterinarians cannot ask their patients whether and where they are experiencing discomfort. Additionally, veterinarians must be aware of the survival instinct of many animals to mask pain in response to stressful experiences or foreign environments. For these reasons, diagnostic tools and strategies are instrumental in the effective practice of veterinary medicine.

Why is it easier for doctors to diagnose painful illnesses and injuries than it is for veterinarians?

The chemical elements in water, hydrogen and oxygen, are some of the most abundant elements in the universe. Astronomers see the signature of water in giant molecular clouds between the stars, in disks of material that represent newborn planetary systems, and in the atmospheres of giant planets orbiting other stars. There are several worlds thought to possess liquid water beneath their surfaces, and many more that have water in the form of ice or vapor.

Why might astronomers be interested in finding water on planets other than Earth?

Five icy moons of Jupiter and Saturn show strong evidence of oceans beneath their surfaces: Ganymede, Europa and Callisto at Jupiter, and Enceladus and Titan at Saturn. Scientists using NASA's Hubble Space Telescope recently provided powerful evidence that Ganymede has a saltwater, sub-surface ocean, likely sandwiched between two layers of ice. Europa and Enceladus are each thought to have an ocean of liquid water beneath its surface in contact with mineral-rich rock.

Which moon has a saltwater ocean, in scientists' opinion, and why might scientists be interested in a saltwater ocean?

Doctors' patients are humans, who can tell their doctors "whether and where they are experiencing discomfort." Obviously, animals cannot use language to communicate with vets.

Because planets with water might also be inhabited with living creatures.

Scientists think Jupiter's moon Ganymede "has a saltwater, sub-surface ocean, likely sandwiched between two layers of ice." A saltwater ocean might interest scientists because Earth has saltwater oceans.

It's easy to forget that the story of Earth's water, from gentle rains to raging rivers, is intimately connected to the larger story of our solar system and beyond. But our water came from somewhere—every world in our solar system got its water from the same shared source. So it's worth considering that the next glass of water you drink could easily have been part of a comet, or an ocean moon, or a long-vanished sea on the surface of Mars.

How does the author seem to feel about the information in this passage?

At sunset especially did we most enjoy the magnificent sight of the lake, which could be seen from my windows in its whole length. An orange light then stained the west at the place where the mountains of Savoy dip down into the lake. These mountains stood out boldly against the blazing horizon. At the right a purple zone crowned the hills and grew feebler toward the town of Vevey; in the midst of the lake flamed a marvelous fire....

What is this passage's tone?

Gulliver's Travels was published in 1726, and the book was soon appropriated by the children, who have ever since continued to regard it as one of the most delightful of their story books. They cannot comprehend the occasion which provoked the book nor appreciate the satire which underlies the narrative, but they delight in the wonderful adventures, and wander full of open-eyed aston-ishment into the new worlds through which the vivid and logically accurate imagination of the author so personally conducts them.

Is this author expressing facts or opinions? How do you know?

The author seems awed by the fact that Earth's water—in fact, our drinking water—probably came from "part of a comet, or an ocean moon, or a long-vanished sea on the surface of Mars."

It has an admiring, awestruck tone.

He or she is expressing opinions about children's reactions to the novel *Gulliver's Travels*. Except for the book's publishing date, the author cannot prove any of the statements made in this book.

It wasn't until microwave popcorn became commercially available in 1981 that at-home popcorn consumption began to grow exponentially. With the wide availability of microwaves in the United States, popcorn also began popping up in offices and hotel rooms. However, the home still remains the most popular popcorn eating spot: today, 70 percent of the 16 billion quarts of popcorn consumed annually in the United States are eaten at home.

Why did "at-home popcorn consumption [begin] to grow exponentially" in 1981?

A fault of disproportionate height of ceilings must be avoided when renovating a house. During the renovation of an old house with high ceilings, walls are added to divide the original, but very large, rooms. In a modern house, if one room is large enough to require a lofty ceiling, the architect will manage to make his second floor upon different levels, so as not to inflict the necessary height of large rooms upon narrow halls and small rooms, which should have only a height proportioned to their size.

What is the author's main purpose for writing this passage?

The reduced ozone concentrations resulting from a nuclear "exchange" would have a number of consequences outside the areas in which the detonations occurred. The Academy study notes, for example, that the resultant increase in ultraviolet would cause "prompt incapacitating cases of sunburn in the temperate zones and snow blindness in northern countries . . ."

Strange though it might seem, the increased ultraviolet radiation could also be accompanied by a drop in the average temperature.

Why does the author include the phrase "strange as it may seem"?

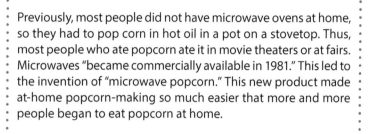

Previously, most people did not have microwave ovens at home, so they had to pop corn in hot oil in a pot on a stovetop. Thus, most people who ate popcorn ate it in movie theaters or at fairs. Microwaves "became commercially available in 1981." This led to the invention of "microwave popcorn." This new product made at-home popcorn-making so much easier that more and more people began to eat popcorn at home.

The author wants to teach readers his or her opinions about renovating a house. The author is probably an expert on this topic. However, the passage expresses opinions, not facts.

Most people would probably assume that "increased ultraviolet radiation" would lead the average temperature to soar, not drop.

During the 1920s in the United States, jazz music provided the soundtrack for the explosion of African American art and culture now known as the Harlem Renaissance. In addition to Ella Fitzgerald and Louis Armstrong, numerous musicians, including Duke Ellington, Fats Waller, and Bessie Smith, promoted their distinctive and complex music as an integral part of the emerging African American culture.

How did jazz music affect the Harlem Renaissance?

A classic, according to the usual definition, is an old author canonized by admiration, and an authority in his particular style. The word classic was first used in this sense by the Romans. With them not all the citizens of the different classes were properly called *classici*, but only those of the chief class, those who possessed an income of a certain fixed sum. Those who possessed a smaller income were described by the term infra *classem*, below the pre-eminent class.

Use context to define the word *canonized* in the passage.

Keep an eye on unpaid student loans, medical bills, and parking tickets, all of which can take a negative toll on your credit score. In fact, your credit score will take a major hit from any bill that's sent to a collection agency, so it's in your best interest to avoid letting bills get to that point. Many organizations will agree to keep bills away from collection agencies if you set up a fee payment system.

What does a collection agency do?

Jazz music formed an important part of the Harlem Renaissance and "provided the soundtrack" for this cultural "explosion." During this time, most jazz musicians were African American; the Harlem Renaissance was an African American cultural movement centered in Harlem, a neighborhood in New York City.

In this passage, *canonized* probably means "idolized" or "revered."

It tries to collect overdue bills from people who owe money; it works for companies that lend people money.

In ancient Rome, the word *classicus* was used in a figurative sense by Aulus Gellius, and applied to writers: a writer of worth and distinction, *classicus assiduusque* scripter, a writer who is of account, has real property, and is not lost in the proletariat crowd. Such an expression implies an age sufficiently advanced to have already made some sort of valuation and classification of literature.

In this passage, what does the phrase "of account" mean?

Idealists of the Romantic Era saw a connection between ideals and nature. In fact, some Romantics asserted that the "natural instincts" of life are often expressions of truth. The desire to be free is a natural tendency of creation.

Who believed that "the desire to be free is a natural tendency of creation"?

Mind, in this speech I have been trying merely to do honor to the New England weather—no language could do it justice. But, after all, there is at least one or two things about that weather (or, if you please, effects produced by it) which we residents would not like to part with. If we hadn't our bewitching autumn foliage, we should still have to credit the weather with one feature which compensates for all its bullying vagaries—the ice-storm....

Which aspects of the weather in New England is Twain praising? About which aspects is he complaining?

The phrase "of account" probably means "worthy of admiration." Maybe the author is saying that such a writer's written works are worthy of admiration.

"Idealists of the Romantic Era" believed that this was so.

He seems to be praising the "bewitching autumn foliage" and "the ice-storm." He seems to be complaining about the weather's "bullying vagaries."

Human behavior cannot be understood in a vacuum; that is, our daily behaviors are inextricably linked with the social context in which they occur. Why is this important? According to social psychologist Eliot Aronson, it's important because it helps us to understand that the behaviors we witness in others may be as much a result of social influence as they are of the individual's disposition.

Why might it be important to know that someone's behavior might be caused by "social influence" rather than by that "individual's disposition"?

...ice that is as bright and clear as crystal; when every bough and twig is strung with ice-beads, frozen dew-drops, and the whole tree sparkles cold and white, like the Shah of Persia's diamond plume. Then the wind waves the branches and the sun comes out and turns all those myriads of beads and drops to prisms that glow and burn and flash with all manner of colored fires, which change and change again with inconceivable rapidity from blue to red, from red to green, and green to gold....

What is the author's tone and purpose in this passage?

...and the sun comes out and turns all those myriads of [frozen] beads and drops to prisms that glow and burn and flash with all manner of colored fires, which change and change again with inconceivable rapidity from blue to red, from red to green, and green to gold—the tree becomes a spraying fountain, a very explosion of dazzling jewels; and it stands there the acme, the climax, the supremest possibility in art or nature, of bewildering, intoxicating, intolerable magnificence. One cannot make the words too strong.

In the last sentence, what is Twain's tone?

Answers may vary. Example: If people behave in a problematic way (for example, if they break the law), and we know their bad behavior is to some degree caused by society, we might be able to make societal changes that may change this bad behavior.

In this passage, Mark Twain seems delighted and awestruck by the beauty of nature. His purpose is to delight his readers/ listeners and to attempt to re-create the beauty of the scene with precise descriptive language.

His tone is absolutely sincere: he truly believes what he is saying. He truly believes that the scene he has described is "the supremest possibility in art or nature, of bewildering, intoxicating, intolerable magnificence."

Animals do not necessarily tolerate pain any better than humans do, though they may handle their pain differently. Dr. Debbie Grant emphasizes that veterinarians must be aware that a lack of obvious signs does not necessarily suggest that pain is not present: in fact, many animals, especially those that are prey animals in the wild, are likely to conceal their pain out of an instinct to hide weaknesses that may make them easy targets for predators.

Why are "prey animals in the wild . . . likely to conceal their pain"?

William James, 1842 – 1910, was an influential American philosopher and psychologist who studied the human psyche. He taught that the function of thought is to guide action; his central focus was practical effects of knowledge. James urges teachers to use the principles suggested by psychology, the science of the mind, as guidelines in the same way the science of logic or ethics offers a set of standards or rules to help govern specific choices.

What is the author's main purpose in this passage?

It is painfully evident, upon experiment, that not many of the books which come teeming from our presses every year are meant to be read. They are meant, it may be, to be pondered; it is hoped, no doubt, they may instruct, or inform, or startle, or arouse, or reform, or provoke, or amuse us; but we read, if we have the true reader's zest and plate, not to grow more knowing, but to be less pent up and bound within a little circle....

What does the word *teeming* mean here? What is Wilson's tone in this passage?

They conceal their pain because they have "an instinct to hide weaknesses that may make them easy targets for predators."

The author's main purpose is to inform readers about William James's philosophies.

Here, teeming means "coming in great numbers." Wilson's tone is instructive and serious: he is trying to make an important point about books and reading.

...we read, if we have the true reader's zest and plate, not to grow more knowing, but to be less pent up and bound within a little circle,—, and not as those who laboriously seek instruction,—as a means of seeing and enjoying the world of men and affairs. We wish companionship and renewal of spirit, enrichment of thought and the full adventure of the mind; and we desire fair company, and a larger world in which to find them.

In Wilson's opinion, why does a "true reader" read?

Some books remain with you, and will not be forgotten or laid by. They cling like a personal experience, and become the mind's intimates. You devour a book meant to be read, not because you would fill yourself or have an anxious care to be nourished, but because it contains such stuff as it makes the mind hungry to look upon. Neither do you read it to kill time, but to lengthen time, rather, adding to its natural usury by living the more abundantly while it lasts, joining another's life and thought to your own.

What is this passage's main idea?

The Constitution says: "We, the people of the United States, in order to form a more perfect union...."

It was we, the people; not we, the white male citizens; nor yet we, the male citizens; but we, the whole people, who formed the Union. And we formed it, not to give the blessings of liberty, but to secure them; not to the half of ourselves and the half of our posterity, but to the whole people—women as well as men.

What is Anthony's main argument in this passage?

He believes that a "true reader" reads "to be less pent up and bound within a little circle," for "companionship and renewal of spirit, enrichment of thought and the full adventure of the mind . . . fair company, and a larger world. . . ." In other words, Wilson thinks "true read[ing]" is a great, stimulating pleasure that opens people's minds and releases them from their lives' "little circle[s]."

This passage is mainly about how pleasurable and fulfilling reading can be.

She argues that when the Constitution says "we, the people," it means all the people, not just "the male citizens."

In recent decades, scientific inquiry and urbanization have given birth to a new perspective on the human relationship with animal species. Studies into the common biology and ancestral origins of humans and animals, coupled with the increasing popularity of companion animals over working animals, have led scientists and laymen alike to wonder about the mental and emotional lives of other species. Concerns about animal suffering, for example, have led to major changes in a variety of industries from entertainment to food production.

Why has a "new perspective" recently developed on "the human relationship with animal[s]"?

Scientists think it was too hot in the solar system's early days for water to condense into liquid or ice on the inner planets, so it had to be delivered—possibly by comets and water-bearing asteroids. NASA's Dawn mission is currently studying Ceres, which is the largest body in the asteroid belt between Mars and Jupiter. Researchers think Ceres might have a water-rich composition similar to some of the bodies that brought water to the three rocky, inner planets, including Earth.

How do scientists think Earth originally got its water?

Martin Seligman's 2011 book is titled *Flourish: A Visionary New Understanding of Happiness and Well-being.* The author's well-being theory addresses not only life satisfaction but also the extent to which one flourishes in his or her life. According to this theory, an individual's well-being is determined by—in addition to subjective experiences like positive emotions, engagement, and meaning—external factors like constructive relationships and personal achievement.

According to Seligman, which "external factors" help an individual to flourish?

Several factors have contributed to this new perspective; they include "scientific inquiry and urbanization" and "the increasing popularity of companion animals over working animals."

They think Earth's water "had to be delivered—possibly by comets and water-bearing asteroids." They think Earth originally had no water because "it was too hot in the solar system's early days for water to condense into liquid or ice on the inner planets."

"External factors like constructive relationships and personal achievement" help an individual to flourish.

Though positive psychology is a relatively young field within the social sciences, it has already made great strides in attracting attention from researchers and practitioners in the field. Further, it has already begun to gain popular attention, proving that it is on its way to meeting the goal that Dr. Seligman initially set out to accomplish—to have a positive impact on the lives of everyday people who might otherwise have no motivation to seek therapy.

What does the author mean by "a relatively young field"?

On the fifth of November, which was the beginning of summer in those parts, the weather being very hazy, the seamen spied a rock within half a cable's length of the ship; but the wind was so strong, that we were driven directly upon it, and immediately split. Six of the crew, of whom I was one, having let down the boat into the sea, made a shift to get clear of the ship and the rock. We rowed, by my computation, about three leagues....

Where and when is this scene from the novel set?

Credit scores are used by many institutions that need to evaluate the risk of providing loans, rentals, or services to individuals. Banks use credit scores when deciding whether to hand out loans; they can also use them to determine the terms of the loan itself. Similarly, car dealers, landlords, and credit card companies will likely all access your credit report before agreeing to do business with you. Even your employer can access a modified version of your credit report.

What is this passage's main idea?

The author means that "positive psychology" developed recently.

It is set at sea in November.

The main idea is expressed in the first sentence: "Credit scores are used by many institutions that need to evaluate the risk of providing loans, rentals, or services to individuals." The other sentences in the passage tell more about this main idea.

We rowed, by my computation, about three leagues, till we were able to work no longer, being already spent with labor, while we were in the ship. We, therefore, trusted ourselves to the mercy of the waves; and, in about half an hour, the boat was overset by a sudden flurry from the north. What became of my companions in the boat, as well as those who escaped on the rock, or were left in the vessel, I cannot tell, but conclude they were all lost.

What happens to the narrator in this part of the novel?

Being smart about taking on debt is a key factor in keeping your credit score high. If you are just starting off in the financial world, there will be multiple offers to open accounts, say, for an introductory credit card or short-term loan. But just because banks are offering you those loans doesn't make them a good idea. Instead, you should only take on debt you know you can pay back in a reasonable amount of time.

What is the author's main purpose for writing this passage?

"Castle/Bravo" was the largest nuclear weapon ever detonated by the United States. Before it was set off at Bikini on February 28, 1954, it was expected to explode with an energy equivalent of about 8 million tons of TNT. Actually, it produced almost twice that explosive power—equivalent to 15 million tons of TNT.

If the power of the bomb was unexpected, so were the after-effects. About 6 hours after the explosion, a fine, sandy ash began to sprinkle the Japanese fishing vessel Lucky Dragon, some 90 miles downwind of the burst point....

How does the author seem to feel?

He and his companions are in a rowboat that is "overset." All his companions drown, apparently. The narrator (since he is still telling the story) is presumably still alive.

To warn people not to take on debt if they cannot "pay [these debts] back in a reasonable amount of time."

Readers cannot really tell how the author feels about the denotation. He or she mainly just reports the facts.

If we hadn't our bewitching autumn foliage, we should still have to credit the weather with one feature which compensates for all its bullying vagaries—the ice-storm: when a leafless tree is clothed with ice from the bottom to the top—ice that is as bright and clear as crystal; when every bough and twig is strung with ice-beads, frozen dew-drops, and the whole tree sparkles cold and white, like the Shah of Persia's diamond plume.

What is this passage's main theme?

What became of my companions in the boat ... I cannot tell, but conclude they were all lost.

For my own part, I swam as fortune directed me, and was pushed forward by wind and tide. I often let my legs drop, and could feel no bottom; but, when I was almost gone, and able to struggle no longer, I found myself within my depth; and, by this time, the storm was much abated.

What happens to the narrator in this part of the novel?

The only question left to be settled now is: Are women persons? And I hardly believe any of our opponents will have the hardihood to say they are not. Being persons, then, women are citizens; and no state has a right to make any law... that shall abridge their privileges... Hence, every discrimination against women in the constitutions and laws of the several states is today null and void, precisely as is every one against [African Americans].

Why does Anthony compare women to African Americans here? What point is she making?

Its main theme is the beauty of nature in general and the beauty of an ice-storm in particular.

He and his companions have fallen out of a boat on the sea. He concludes that his companions have drowned. He swims and floats until he is almost exhausted. Finally, he "[finds himself] within [his] depth"—in other words, he can touch the sea bottom with his feet and still keep his head above water.

In 1873, when Anthony made this speech, African American men (some of them) had only recently gained the right to vote. Anthony's point is that women should have equal rights with these new voters because they are all "persons" and citizens.

...I walked near a mile before I got to the shore, which I conjectured was about eight o'clock in the evening. I then advanced forward near half a mile, but could not discover any sign of houses or inhabitants; at least, I was in so weak a condition, that I did not observe them. I was extremely tired, and with that, and the heat of the weather, and about half a pint of brandy that I drank as I left the ship, I found myself much inclined to sleep.

Where is this scene set? What does the narrator do?

It has now been two decades since the introduction of thermonuclear fusion weapons into the military inventories of the great powers, and more than a decade since the United States, Great Britain, and the Soviet Union ceased to test nuclear weapons in the atmosphere. Today our understanding of the technology of thermonuclear weapons seems highly advanced, but our knowledge of the physical and biological consequences of nuclear war is continuously evolving.

What is another (shorter) way to say "thermonuclear fusion weapons"?

William James, 1842 – 1910, urges teachers to use the principles suggested by psychology, the science of the mind, as guidelines in the same way the science of logic or ethics offers a set of standards or rules to help govern specific choices. The three principles include: First, engage the interest of students by determining what they need to know and being aware of what they already know and what they do not know. Second, make what is presented memorable. Third, build student curiosity about what will be next.

What is this passage's main idea? Describe one important detail.

The scene is apparently set on a coastline with water that is shallow enough to walk in. The narrator walks to shore, looks for houses and people, and realizes how exhausted he is.

A shorter way to say this is "nuclear weapons."

Main idea: as part of his philosophy on teaching, William James presented three principals. Detail: James's second principle was that teachers should "make [what they present to students] memorable."

Only recently, new light was shed on the subject of nuclear war in a study which the Arms Control and Disarmament Agency had asked the National Academy of Sciences to undertake. Previous studies had tended to focus very largely on radioactive fallout from a nuclear war; an important aspect of this new study was its inquiry into all possible consequences, including the effects of large-scale nuclear detonations on the ozone layer which helps protect life on earth from the sun's ultraviolet radiations.

What effect would "large-scale nuclear detonations" probably have on Earth's "ozone layer"?

Assuming...a large-scale but less than total nuclear "exchange," as one would say in the dehumanizing jargon of the strategists—it was concluded that as much as 30–70 percent of the ozone might be eliminated from the northern hemisphere (where a nuclear war would presumably take place) and as much as 20–40 percent from the southern hemisphere. Recovery would probably take about 3–10 years, but the Academy's study notes that long term global changes cannot be completely ruled out.

Explain why the author thinks the expression "nuclear exchange" is an example of "dehumanizing jargon."

Water is found in primitive bodies like comets and asteroids, and dwarf planets like Ceres. The atmospheres and interiors of the four giant planets—Jupiter, Saturn, Uranus and Neptune—are thought to contain enormous quantities of the wet stuff, and their moons and rings have substantial water ice.

Perhaps the most surprising water worlds are the five icy moons of Jupiter and Saturn that show strong evidence of oceans beneath their surfaces: Ganymede, Europa and Callisto at Jupiter, and Enceladus and Titan at Saturn.

How many of Saturn's moons are "icy"?

Nuclear detonations would probably have a very harmful effect on the ozone layer, and this would expose "life on earth [to] the sun's ultraviolet radiations." This, in turn, could cause millions of people, animals, and plant species to die.

The word *exchange* sounds a lot more harmless and neutral than an actual nuclear war would be: such a war would cause unimaginable death and suffering.

Two: Enceladus and Titan.

Understanding the distribution of water in our solar system tells us a great deal about how the planets, moons, comets and other bodies formed 4.5 billion years ago from the disk of gas and dust that surrounded our sun. The space closer to the sun was hotter and drier than the space farther from the sun, which was cold enough for water to condense.

Do the planets closest to our sun have water on them?

The amount of water in the giant planet Jupiter holds a critical missing piece to the puzzle of our solar system's formation. Jupiter was likely the first planet to form, and it contains most of the material that wasn't incorporated into the sun. The leading theories about its formation rest on the amount of water the planet soaked up.

Do scientists think Jupiter "soaked up" a great deal of water, only a little, or none? What makes you think so?

"Castle/Bravo" was the largest nuclear weapon ever detonated by the United States. it was expected to explode with an energy equivalent of about 8 million tons of TNT. Actually, it produced almost twice that explosive power. More than any other event in the decade of testing large nuclear weapons in the atmosphere, Castle/Bravo's unexpected contamination of 7,000 square miles of the Pacific Ocean dramatically illustrated how large-scale nuclear war could produce casualties on a colossal scale, far beyond the local effects of blast and fire alone.

How does the author seem to feel about the "decade of testing large nuclear weapons"?

The planets closest to our sun probably do not have water because it is too hot and dry there. The passage says that "the space farther from the sun . . . was cold enough for water to condense."

They probably think Jupiter "soaked up" a great deal of water. The passage says that Jupiter is a "giant planet," and that it was "likely the first planet to form, and it contains most of the material that wasn't incorporated into the sun." This implies that it "soaked up" a lot of the water that first existed in our solar system.

It is a little difficult to tell how the author feels, since he or she mostly just reports the facts; however, the author does seem awed and frightened by the prospect of a "large-scale nuclear war [that] could produce casualties on a colossal scale."

Throughout the bloody series of French and Indian wars which ravaged the frontier settlements of America during the first half of the eighteenth century, France maintained secure possession of the regions of the great lakes and the basin of the upper Mississippi. The successful campaign of the gallant Wolfe against the no-less-gallant Montcalm ultimately resulted in the termination of French supremacy in these sections, and under the treaty of Paris, in 1763, Canada with all other dominions of France east of the Mississippi passed into the control of Great Britain.

Was Wolfe British or French?

In 1763, Canada, with all other dominions of France east of the Mississippi, passed into the control of Great Britain. To this time the English colonists had confined their operations almost entirely to the region of the Atlantic Coast, so when Great Britain acquired her immense war-inheritance, the country to the west of the Appalachian Mountain range was practically an unknown region to its new masters.

Explain how "the English colonists" because the "new masters" to "the country to the west of the Appalachian Mountain range."

He was British. Wolfe's campaign was successful, while Mont-calm's was not: Britain won and France lost. The author believes that both leaders were equally "gallant," however.

When Great Britain won a war, this region "passed into the control" of England. Since the English colonists were Englishmen, they could now be "masters" of the region.

2

Writing

What is the difference between a proper noun and a common noun?

Are the words *am*, *is*, and *are* verbs? Why or why not?

A proper noun is capitalized; it names a certain person, place, or thing. Examples: Barack Obama, Los Angeles, the Rock of Gibraltar. A common noun is usually not capitalized; it names more than one person, place, or thing. Examples: captain, highway, boulder.

Yes, they are "verbs of being," forms of the verb *to be*. Not all verbs express action.

What is a proper adjective?

What are the seven coordinating conjunctions?

Which two words in the following sentence are prepositions?
My cat usually sleeps on the bed with me.

It is a capitalized adjective that refers to a certain person, place, or thing, and modifies a noun. Examples: in the term *African American*, *African* is a proper adjective that modifies the proper noun *American*; in the term *Belgian waffle*, *Belgian* is a proper adjective that modifies the common noun *waffle*.

and, or, but, nor, so, for, yet

on and *with*

Which word in the following sentence is an interjection?

Wow, what is that horrible smell?

How can you tell if a sentence is complete?

Which words in the following sentence form an adjective phrase?

The woman on the bus wore a uniform.

Wow

A complete sentence expresses a complete thought. It contains at least one subject (a noun or noun phrase) and at least one predicate (a verb or verb phrase).

"On the bus" is an adjective phrase that modifies the noun *woman*.

Which words in the following sentence form a dependent clause (also known as a subordinate clause)?

When it started to rain, we ran indoors.

What is the purpose of a declarative sentence, and with what punctuation mark does it usually end?

What is the main difference between a comma and a semicolon?

"When it started to rain"

A declarative sentence (like this one) makes a statement; it usually ends with a period.

A comma indicates a short pause, and a semicolon indicates a longer pause. In a compound sentence, a semicolon can take the place of a comma followed by a conjunction. Example: *My cat has annoying habits; for example, she likes to sit in front of my computer screen.*

What is wrong with the expression
"I could care less"?

What is wrong with the
following sentence?

*Excellent movies, such as Cocoon,
Parenthood, and Apollo 13 reveals
director Ron Howard's gift for
portraying life in the United States.*

How can a run-on sentence be corrected?

The correct expression is "I *couldn't* care less." It means "I don't care at all." If you *could* care less about something, then you *do* care about it.

The singular verb *reveals* does not agree with its plural subject, *movies*. The verb should be changed to *reveal*.

A run-on sentence can be fixed by 1) inserting a comma and a conjunction; 2) inserting a semicolon; or 3) rewriting the run-on sentence as two sentences.

Read this sentence and identify the misspelled word or words.

Their standing right over there with they're parents.

In the sentence *I threw the ball to Pablo*, which pronoun could you substitute for Pablo's name?

Carrying a heavy backpack, I walked up the steep, dusty trail in 90-degree weather.

What verb could you substitute for *walked* to make the sentence more descriptive?

The first word in the sentence, *Their*, should be spelled *They're* (or *They are*). The second-to-last word, *they're*, should be spelled *their*.

him

Examples: *hiked, trudged, tramped, plodded, slogged*

What are the main differences between adjectives and adverbs?

In the following sentence, is the word *because* a coordinating conjunction or a subordinating conjunction?

I dislike fresh tomatoes because they have a squishy texture.

In the phrase "lying peacefully on the comfortable couch," which word is a preposition?

An adjective modifies a noun or a pronoun. Examples: *a gorgeous sunset*; *she is courageous*. An adverb modifies a verb, an adjective, or another adverb. Examples: *to amble lazily; amazingly beautiful; to speak incredibly quietly.*

Because is a subordinating conjunction; it introduces a subordinate clause ("because they have a squishy texture") and connects it to the sentence's main clause ("I dislike fresh tomatoes").

on

Which word in the following sentence is an interjection?

As I lay there, I thought to myself, hey, aren't I supposed to be somewhere at noon today?

Which word or words in this sentence form a direct object?

I quickly read the third chapter.

Which words in the following sentence form an adverb phrase?

While I was running around Green Lake, I saw Gary Grenell, a local photographer.

hey

chapter or "the third chapter"

"around Green Lake"

Which words in the following sentence form the main clause (also known as an independent clause)?

Although I like uncooked raisins, I do not like them in cookies, cinnamon rolls, or hot cereal.

What is the purpose of an interrogative sentence, and with what punctuation mark does this type of sentence end?

Which punctuation mark in the following sentence could be replaced by a colon (:)?

Let me tell you something important— never carry your Social Security number in your wallet!

"I do not like them in cookies, cinnamon rolls, or hot cereal."

An interrogative sentence asks a question; it ends with a question mark.

The em dash could be replaced by a colon, as seen in the following sentence.

Let me tell you something important: never carry your Social Security number in your wallet!

What is wrong with the following sentence?

I am so excited about this project that my head is literally exploding with ideas.

What is wrong with the following sentence?

My mom, my sister, and even my dad enjoys cooking huge family dinners on weekends.

What is a comma splice, and how can it be corrected?

The adverb *literally* means "actually, really, in fact." You can't truthfully say your head is "literally exploding" unless it is *actually* exploding (in which case you probably wouldn't be able to say or write anything).

The singular verb *enjoys* does not agree with its plural subject, "my mom, my sister, and even my dad." The verb should be changed to *enjoy*.

A comma splice is an incorrectly-written compound sentence in which there is a comma but no conjunction connecting two shorter complete sentences. A comma splice can be fixed by 1) inserting a conjunction after the comma, 2) replacing the comma with a semicolon, or 3) rewriting the sentence as two sentences.

Read this sentence, identify the misspelled word, and spell it correctly.

I was surprised to find that in the past year, my younger cousin has grown taller then I am.

Complete the following sentence with *one* pronoun.

_____ all live together at 2145 Basil Lane.

In the following sentence, which verb has a direct object? Which one or two words comprise the direct object?

Purring loudly, the mother cat grooms her kittens with her rough tongue.

The third-to-last word, *then*, should be spelled *than*.

We or *They*

The verb *grooms* has a direct object: *kittens* or "her kittens." (The verb *purring* does not have a direct object.)

In the following sentence, identify one adverb and one adjective.

Sleeping on the floor can be amazingly comfortable.

In the sentence *I like baked potatoes, but I love French fries*, is the word *but* a coordinating conjunction or a subordinating conjunction?

Identify two prepositional phrases in the following sentence.

My family and I used to camp in the Wawona Campground at Yosemite National Park.

Adverb: *amazingly*; adjective: *comfortable*

But is a coordinating conjunction; it connects two short—but complete—sentences. ("I like baked potatoes" and "I love French fries"). Neither short sentence is a subordinate clause.

1) "in the Wawona Campground; 2) "at Yosemite National Park"

Which one of these words is NOT
an interjection?

Which two words in this sentence form
the sentence's subject?
Thinking aloud may not be wise.

Which word in the following sentence is a
helping verb? Also identify the verb that
the helping verb "helps."
Might you need help from Matty and me?

hey, wow, oh, painful, hooray, ouch
The word *painful* is an adjective, not an interjection.

"Thinking aloud"

The helping verb is *might*; it "helps" (modifies) the verb *need*, as in "you <u>might need</u> help."

Which words in the following sentence form the main clause (independent clause), and which form the subordinate clause (dependent clause)?

While I would love to attend the conference, the decision is up to my supervisor.

What is the purpose of an exclamation, and with what punctuation mark does this type of sentence usually end?

What punctuation mark is missing from the following sentence, and where does the missing mark belong?

My mom stared at me and exclaimed, "You have got to be kidding!

The main clause is: "the decision is up to my supervisor." The subordinate clause is: "While I would love to attend the conference."

An exclamation expresses strong emotion; it usually ends with an exclamation mark. Example: *Wow, I just love riding on rollercoasters!*

The sentence is missing a closing quotation mark; it belongs at the very end of the sentence, after the exclamation mark.

The following sentence might work fine in an informal conversation or a friendly email. However, it uses language that is inappropriate for formal writing. How might you restate the following to make it sound more formal?

Addy was all like,
"Shut UP! Are you serious?"

What is wrong with the following sentence?

That is a flimsy explanation which do not adequately excuse their actions.

What is a rambling sentence?
Is a rambling sentence
always ungrammatical?

Addy was amazed when I told her the news. She said, "I can't believe it! Are you sure it's true?"

The plural helping verb *do* does not agree with its singular subject, *explanation*. *Do* should be replaced with *does*.

A rambling sentence is one that goes on and on in a tedious way; it is impossible to read aloud in one breath. Not all rambling sentences are ungrammatical.

**Identify two misspelled words
and spell them correctly.**

*Why didn't you tell me that your leaving on
a two-week visit to you're grandmother?*

**Complete the following sentence
with *one* pronoun.**

*I hope my grandparents will be in shape
for their bicycle trip this summer—
I don't want them to injure _____.*

**In the following sentence, which verb
has an indirect object? Which one or two
words comprise the indirect object?**

*I yawned, stretched, scratched a
mosquito bite on my arm,
and gave my dog her breakfast.*

The seventh word, *your*, should be spelled *you're*. The second-to-last word, *you're*, should be spelled *your*.

themselves

The verb *gave* has an indirect object: *dog* or "my dog."

In the following sentence, identify one adverb and one adjective.

I will be everlastingly grateful to you if you do me this favor.

Although November is usually my favorite month of the year, this year it rained too much for me.

Is the word *although* a coordinating conjunction or a subordinating conjunction?

What is the purpose of an imperative sentence, and with which punctuation mark(s) does this type of sentence usually end?

Adverb: *everlastingly*; adjective: *grateful*

Although is a subordinating conjunction; it connects a subordinate clause ("Although November is usually my favorite month of the year") to the sentence's main clause ("this year it rained too much for me").

An imperative sentence is a command; it usually ends with a period or an exclamation mark. Examples: *Follow the directions at the top of your test sheet. Set the table right NOW!*

FIND THE ERROR:

Not every nation has a President as its leader; some have prime ministers, some have kings or queens, and others have military dictators.

FIND THE ERROR:

In our club, everyone who attends the meetings stay afterward to help clean up.

FIND THE ERROR:

I love French Fries, Belgian waffles, and Italian pasta.

In this sentence, *president* is a common noun (a noun that names more than one person), so it should not be capitalized.

The plural verb *stay* does not agree with its singular subject, *everyone*. *Stay* should be replaced with *stays*.

Even though the proper adjective *French* is capitalized, the common noun *fries* should be lowercased.

FIND THE ERROR:
First we will fly to Copenhagen, a port city in Denmark and then we will board a ship and sail to several different Baltic nations.

FIND THE ERROR:
Whenever I scratch my dog's belly, she grins over joy.

FIND THE ERROR:
What is that delicious—wow!—scent wafting out of the kitchen?

This compound sentence needs a comma inserted after *Denmark* and before the conjunction *and*.

The preposition *over* is incorrectly used here; it should be replaced with *with*. Alternatively, the phrase "over joy" might be replaced with *joyfully*.

The interjection *wow* is incorrectly placed in the sentence; it interrupts the sentence's flow. *Wow* should be moved to the beginning of the sentence and followed by a comma. Alternatively, this interjection could form a one-word exclamation by itself: *Wow! What is that delicious scent wafting out of the kitchen?*

FIND THE ERROR:

It is Ana's birthday next Wednesday, we're planning a family celebration for the following weekend.

FIND THE ERROR:

The two older people are Shelby's great-grandparents standing over there.

FIND THE ERROR:

I would love to attend your dinner party, my wife has made other plans for the night of the 12th.

This is an incorrectly constructed sentence (a comma splice). It needs a conjunction such as *so* or *and* following the comma and before the word *we're*.

The adjective phrase "standing over there" is misplaced in the sentence. It should be moved to follow the noun it modifies, *people*: *The two older people <u>standing over there</u> are Shelby's great-grandparents.*

This sentence is incorrectly constructed (it is a comma splice). It needs a subordinating conjunction such as *While* or *Although* at the beginning of the clause "I would love to attend your dinner party." Alternatively, the conjunction *but* could be inserted after the comma and before the word *my*.

FIND THE ERROR:

Alexander Hamilton, whose portrait is on the twenty-dollar bill, was one of our nation's "Founding Fathers"?

FIND THE ERROR:

"Wow;" she exclaimed. "This is one of the best days of my entire life!"

FIND THE ERROR:

Lydia does not agree with this president's policies, so she could care less if his approval rating drops even lower in the polls.

This is a statement (or declarative sentence), so it should end with a period, not a question mark.

The semicolon following *Wow* is incorrect punctuation. This mark should be changed to a comma or an exclamation mark.

The correct expression is "could *not* care less." "Could care less" is incorrect—it conveys the opposite meaning from the one intended.

FIND THE ERROR:

The fact that movies and TV shows based on Jane Austen's completed novels has attracted millions of viewers would have astonished the author, who died 200 years ago.

FIND THE ERROR:

Sometimes I wonder whether I will ever travel to Africa, Asia, South America, or Antarctica—so far, I have never been to any of these continents; however, I live in the United States, I have traveled to Canada and Mexico, and I have been to many nations in Europe, including England, Scotland, Ireland, France, Italy, Switzerland, and Holland.

FIND THE ERROR:

Wow, your lucky to have such a big apartment, and you're patio is so nice and shady!

The singular verb *has attracted* does not agree with its plural subject, *movies*. *Has* should be changed to *have*.

While this sentence is not ungrammatical, it is a rambling sentence and should probably be rewritten. As it stands, it is a sentence that is too long and tedious to read.

The second word, *your*, should be spelled *you're* or "you are." The eleventh word, *you're*, should be spelled *your*.

FIND THE ERROR:

Which State in the United States is larger, Alaska or Texas?

FIND THE ERROR:

Katrina, the youngest of my four cats, are due for a check-up at the vet.

FIND THE ERROR:

You have two choices: you can work overtime to finish the project, and you can tell your supervisor that you cannot meet the deadline.

The second word in the sentence, *State*, should be lowercased; here it functions as a common noun, not as a proper noun.

The plural verb *are* does not agree with its singular subject, *Katrina. Are* should be changed to *is*.

The conjunction *and* should be changed to *or* to indicate a choice; as is, the sentence does not make sense.

FIND THE ERROR:

Alex plans to buy the most big cake he can find for his sister's birthday.

FIND THE ERROR:

We had made an appointment to meet at 2 p.m., so by 2:30 p.m. I began to wonder where Amy was at.

FIND THE ERROR:

Danny stepped on a tack and yelled, "Ouch?" as it pierced his heel.

The superlative form of the adjective *big* is *biggest*, not "most big."

The preposition *at* should be deleted from the end of the sentence; it is not needed.

The question mark following the interjection *Ouch* should be changed to an exclamation mark to show strong emotion (in this case, pain).

FIND THE ERROR:

Can you run to the grocery store tomorrow and pick up some milk and we need eggs, too.

FIND THE ERROR:

On the test people who don't carefully read and follow directions are likely to make mistakes.

FIND THE ERROR:

I can get eight hours of sleep tonight, I don't think I will be able to get up early enough to drive to the city in time for the meeting.

This is a run-on sentence. It can be corrected in more than one way. Two examples: *Can you run to the grocery store tomorrow and pick up some milk and eggs? Can you run to the grocery store tomorrow and pick up some milk? We need eggs, too.*

As is, this sentence is unclear. The phrase "on the test" is meant to modify the noun *mistakes*, so the phrase should be moved to follow this noun: *People who don't carefully read and follow directions are likely to make mistakes on the test.*

This sentence is incorrectly constructed (it is a comma splice), and it does not make sense as is. It needs the subordinating conjunction *Unless* at the beginning of the clause "I can get eight hours of sleep tonight." Alternatively, "I can" might be changed to "If I don't" or "If I cannot."

FIND THE ERROR:

Are you coming with us to Carmina's party this Saturday night.

FIND THE ERROR:

My grandma says that "when she was in high school, she and her classmates handwrote or typed their essays— desktop computers were not common until the late 1980s."

FIND THE ERROR:

I ate so much food on Thanksgiving that my stomach was literally bursting at the seams.

This is a question (or interrogative sentence), so it should end with a question mark, not a period.

This is not a direct quotation, so the quotation marks should be deleted from this sentence. (The speaker is paraphrasing his or her grandmother.)

Since human stomachs do not have seams like clothing or cloth toys, this sentence describes an impossible (and horrifying) scenario. Deleting the word *literally* would make it clear that the writer is using the term "bursting at the seams" figuratively.

FIND THE ERROR:

Only one among the school's 450 students were invited to enter the city's annual spelling bee.

FIND THE ERROR:

Thinking about all the happy and not-so-happy memories from my years in elementary and middle school.

FIND THE ERROR:

For some reason, my family has always ended up living in neighborhoods where most of the other residents own newer, shinier cars then we do.

The plural helping verb *were* does not agree with its singular subject, *one*. *Were* should be changed to *was*.

This is a sentence fragment. One way to complete the sentence might be the following: *That night, as I was falling asleep, I started thinking about all the happy and not-so-happy memories from my years in elementary and middle school.*

The third-to-last word, *then,* should be spelled *than*.

FIND THE ERROR:

Our generous grandparents gave my twin sister and I brand-new bicycles for our birthday.

FIND THE ERROR:

After Mario had camped out in a tent for two weeks, his mattress at home felt delicious soft, and his sheets felt wondrously smooth and clean.

FIND THE ERROR:

In your opinion, which dress is more pretty, the blue silk one or the magenta satin one?

The subject pronoun *I* should be changed to the object pronoun *me*.

The adjective *delicious* should be changed to *deliciously*, an adverb (which modifies the adjective *soft*).

The comparative form of the adjective *pretty* is *prettier*, not "more pretty."

FIND THE ERROR:

I was full after eating a big breakfast, so I ate a huge midmorning snack and a gigantic lunch.

FIND THE ERROR:

No one beside me volunteered to serve on the clean-up committee.

FIND THE ERROR:

Hey who's that knocking on our front door?

The coordinating conjunction *so* does not make sense in this compound sentence. Substituting *yet* or *but* for *so* would clarify the writer's meaning. Alternatively, the sentence could be rewritten as follows: *Even though I was full after eating a big breakfast, I ate a huge midmorning snack and a gigantic lunch.*

Beside is a preposition that means "next to," so it does not make sense here. This word should be changed to *besides*, a preposition that means "except or in addition to." Alternatively, *beside* could be changed to *except*.

The interjection *Hey* should be followed by a comma. Alternatively, the interjection could form its own one-word exclamation: *Hey! Who's that knocking on our front door?*

FIND THE ERROR:

On Friday nights we usually stay home and watch a movie, we sometimes munch on snacks, such as popcorn.

FIND THE ERROR:

From one rooftop to the neighboring one, without pausing to think, to escape the fire, Ben leapt.

FIND THE ERROR:

My movie club meets on Tuesdays, I cannot sign up for a Tuesday/Thursday computer class.

This is a comma splice. It can be corrected in more than one way. Two examples: *On Friday nights we usually stay home, watch a movie, and munch on snacks, such as popcorn. On Friday nights we usually stay home and watch a movie; often we munch on snacks, such as popcorn.*

There are three adverb phrases in this sentence; all three modify the verb *leapt.* If the sentence is to make proper sense, the phrases must be reordered. For example: *To escape the fire, without pausing to think, Ben leapt from one rooftop to the neighboring one.*

This sentence is incorrectly constructed (it is a comma splice). The sentence needs a subordinating conjunction such as *Since* or *Because* at the beginning of the clause "my movie club meets on Tuesdays." Alternatively, the coordinating conjunction *so* could be inserted after the comma and before the pronoun *I.*

FIND THE ERROR:

After you clear the table,
please rinse the dishes and load them
into the dishwasher?

FIND THE ERROR:

Here's what I'd like you to do, tidy up
the living room, dust the furniture, and
vacuum the rug.

FIND THE ERROR:

To many people, promptness and respect
for others are one in the same.

This is a command (or imperative sentence), so it should end with a period, not a question mark.

The first comma in the sentence should be replaced with a colon (:).

The correct expression is "one <u>and</u> the same," not "one <u>in</u> the same."

FIND THE ERROR:
Almost all of the people in my family was planning to attend the reunion.

FIND THE ERROR:
Holly, the woman who works in the front office.

FIND THE ERROR:
There aunt is standing right over there with their parents.

The singular helping verb *was* does not agree with its plural subject, *people*. *Was* should be changed to *were*.

This is a sentence fragment. One way to complete the sentence might be the following: *Holly, the woman who works in the front office, is helpful and friendly to everyone who visits our workplace.*

The first word, *There,* should be spelled *Their* to show possession.

FIND THE ERROR:
I usually give birthday gifts to
she and Jacqueline.

FIND THE ERROR:
All my animals—including my
forty-pound dog—usually sleeps
on my bed at night.

FIND THE ERROR:
The bumblebee bat is the most tiny
mammal in the world.

The subject pronoun *she* should be changed to the object pronoun *her*.

The singular verb *sleeps* does not agree with its plural subject, *animals*. *Sleeps* should be changed to *sleep*.

The superlative form of the adjective *tiny* is *tiniest*, not "most tiny."

FIND THE ERROR:

Whether we were unable to attend the wedding, we sent Mikki and her husband a wedding gift.

FIND THE ERROR:

Wow, that was the most incredible performance I've ever seen.

The coordinating conjunction *Whether* does not make sense in this sentence. Substituting *Although* would clarify the writer's meaning. Alternatively, the sentence could be rewritten as follows: *We were unable to attend the wedding, but we sent Mikki and her husband a wedding gift anyhow.*

This is an exclamation (or an exclamatory sentence), so it should end with an exclamation mark, not a period.

Mathematics

Multiplying a negative number by a
negative number always results in a
_____ number.

What is the commutative property?

positive

The commutative property describes an operation where changing the order does not change the outcome.

$a + b = b + a$

What does the operation "!" do?

What does PEMDAS stand for?

In the number 12,408.57, what place is the number 7 in?

This is factorial: it refers to the product of a number and all the whole numbers below it.

4! = 4 × 3 × 2 × 1 = 24

The order of operations: parentheses, exponents, multiplication/division, and addition/subtraction.

hundredths

What are irrational numbers?

Describe the process for adding and subtracting fractions.

Describe the process for dividing fractions.

Irrational numbers are numbers that cannot be written as fractions.

$e, \pi, \sqrt{3}$

To add or subtract fractions, convert each denominator to the common denominator, add or subtract the numerators, and then simplify the result.

To divide fractions, multiply the first fraction by the reciprocal of the second fraction.

$\frac{a}{b} \div \frac{c}{d} = \frac{a}{b} \times \frac{d}{c} = \frac{ad}{bc}$

What is a prime number?

What is the value of i^2?

In the number 12,408.57, what place is the number 2 in?

a number divisible only by itself and 1

−1
($\sqrt{i} = -1$)

thousand

What is a numerator?

What is a mixed number?

How is a proportion solved?

the number on the top of a fraction

a number with a whole number part and a fraction part

cross-multiply
$\frac{a}{b} = \frac{c}{d} \rightarrow ad = bc$

0! =

What is the formula for increasing or decreasing a number by a percent?

How is a decimal converted to a percent?

0! = 1

---

percent increase = original(1 + percent increase)
percent decrease = original(1 − percent decrease)

---

multiply the decimal by 100
0.37 × 100 = 37%

To simplify the expression 5 + 36 − 2 ÷ 23, which operation is performed first?

What are rational numbers?

What is the distributive property?

The operation inside the parentheses (6 − 2) is performed first.

Rational numbers are numbers that can be written as a fraction.
−4, 1.25, $\frac{4}{3}$

The distributive property is used to multiply a single term by two or more terms inside a set of parentheses.
$a(b + c + d) = ab + ac + ad$

What are positive numbers?

What are negative numbers?

**What is the process for
simplifying square roots?**

numbers greater than 0

numbers less than 0

Rewrite the number under the radical as a product of a perfect square and another number. Then move that root out in front of the radical.

$\sqrt{12} = \sqrt{2^2 \times 3} = 23$

What is an integer?

What are whole numbers?

How is percent difference calculated?

An integer is any number without a decimal part. These include positive and negative numbers, and 0.

..., −2, −1, 0, 1, 2, ...

Whole numbers include both positive integers and 0.

0, 1, 2, 3, 4, 5, ...

percent difference = $\dfrac{\text{new amount} - \text{orginal amount}}{\text{orginal amount}} \times 100$

Describe the process
for multiplying fractions.

What is the associative property?

How can miles per hour be converted
to feet per second?

To multiply fractions, multiply across and simplify.

$$\frac{a}{b} \times \frac{c}{d} = \frac{ac}{bd}$$

The associative property describes an operation where changing the parentheses does not change the outcome.

$$(a + b) + c = a + (b + c)$$

Multiply the original value by the appropriate conversion factors. The original units should cancel, leaving only the new units.

$$\frac{x \text{ miles}}{\text{hour}} \times \frac{5,280 \text{ feet}}{1 \text{ mile}} \times \frac{1 \text{ hour}}{60 \text{ seconds}} = \frac{(x)(5,280) \text{ feet}}{60 \text{ second}}$$

What is the process for writing a number in scientific notation?

$x^0 =$

What are counting numbers?

Place a decimal after the first digit and count the number of places the original decimal needs to be moved. The number of places will be the positive exponent for large numbers, and it will be the negative exponent for numbers less than 1.

$58,300,000 = 5.83 \times 10^7$

$0.00000124 = 1.24 \times 10^{-6}$

$x^0 = 1$

Another name for natural numbers, counting numbers are positive integers.

1, 2, 3, 4, 5, …

What does KHDDCM stand for?

What are the coefficients in the expression $6xy + 3z^2 - 5yz$?

What is the acronym FOIL used for?

KHDDCM is the acronym used for the converting metric units:
<u>K</u>ing <u>H</u>enry <u>D</u>ied <u>D</u>rinking <u>C</u>hocolate <u>M</u>ilk stands for *kilo, hecto, deca, deci, centi, milli.*

6, 3, and 5

to multiply two binomials

FOIL stands for First, Outer, Inner, Last:

$(x + 3)(2x − 5) =$

$2x^2 − 15x + 6x − 15 = 2x^2 − 9x − 15$

F   O   I   L

Which terms in the expression
$3xy^2 + 6xy - 3y^2 - xy^2$
can be added?

What is the point–slope form
of a linear equation?

Which process is the
opposite of factoring?

$3xy^2$ and $-xy^2$

Only terms with the same variables can be added.

point–slope: $y - y_1 = m(x - x_1)$

distributing

What is the formula for finding slope?

What is the slope of a vertical line?

**What is the *y*-intercept
of the line *y* = 3*x* − 2?**

$m = \dfrac{y_2 - y_1}{x_2 - x_1}$

undefined

-2

What does the symbol ≤ mean?

On a number line, the symbol > is
represented by what shape?

When graphing the inequality $y > 4x - 1$,
which side of the line will be shaded?

less than or equal to

an open circle

above the line

What is the intercept form
of a quadratic equation?

What are the zeros (or roots)
of an equation?

Factor $x^2 - y^2$

intercept form: $y = a(x - p)(x - q)$

the x values where the equation crosses the x-axis

$x^2 - y^2 = (x - y)(x + y)$

What is the slope of a horizontal line?

**What is the standard form
of a quadratic equation?**

**What is the vertex form
of a quadratic equation?**

0

standard form: $y = ax^2 + bx + c$

vertex form: $y = a(x - h)^2 + k$

What is the *y*-intercept form
of a linear equation?

Which of the following numbers satisfies
the inequality $0 < x \leq 8$?

What is the standard form
of a linear equation?

y-intercept form: $y = mx + b$

0, 4, 8, 12
4 and 8

standard form: $Ax + By + C = 0$

What are the sides of a 45-45-90 right triangle?

How many points are needed to draw a line?

How many angles are congruent in an equilateral triangle?

The sides of a 45-45-90 right triangle are x, x, and $x\sqrt{2}$.

2

3

Two lines that intersect to form a 90° angle are _____.

What kind of angle is larger than 90°?

Complementary angles add to _____ degrees.

perpendicular

obtuse

90

In a circle, what is the relationship
between the diameter and the radius?

What is the formula for
the circumference of a circle?

Supplementary angles
add to _____ degrees.

The diameter is twice the length of the radius.

$C = 2\pi r$

180

How many degrees are there in a triangle?

The longest distance across
a circle is the _____.

How many sides are congruent
in an isosceles triangle?

180°

diameter

2

How many angles have measurements
greater than 90° in an obtuse triangle?

What is the Pythagorean theorem?

What are the sides of a
30-60-90 right triangle?

1

$c^2 = a^2 + b^2$

The sides of a 30-60-90 right triangle are x, $x\sqrt{3}$, and $2x$.

All of the angles in
a square are _____ degrees.

Which quadrilateral has exactly
one pair of parallel sides?

Which quadrilateral has two pairs of
consecutive equal sides?

90

trapezoid

kite

What is the formula used to calculate the distance between two points?

What is the midpoint formula?

Two lines that lie in the same plane but never intersect are _____.

$$d = \sqrt{(x_2 - x_1)^2 + (y_2 - y_1)^2}$$

$$\left(\frac{x_1 + x_2}{2}, \ \frac{y_1 + y_2}{2} \right)$$

parallel

What is the formula for
the area of a circle?

How many degrees are
there in a quadrilateral?

What are the six types of quadrilaterals?

$A = \pi r^2$

360°

kite, square, rectangle, trapezoid, rhombus, and parallelogram

What is the median of a data set?

Will an outlier have the biggest effect on the value of the mean, median, or mode?

What does the line of best fit of a scatterplot show?

Median is the number in the middle of the set.

Outliers affect mean by shifting it away from the median. Outliers do not affect mode.

The line of best fit shows the general trend of the scatterplot. It shows a positive or negative correlation and the strength of that correlation.

What is the fundamental
counting principle?

What is the difference between
permutations and combinations?

What is the sum of all probabilities in any
probability distribution?

the total number of possible outcomes is the product of the total possible number of outcomes in each trial

For permutations, the order matters; for combinations, the order does not matter.

The sum of all probabilities is always 1.

What is the mean of a data set?

What is the binomial probability formula for *x* successes?

What is a line graph?

Mean is the average value, or the sum of the values divided by the number of values in the set.

$P(X = x) = (p^x)(q^{n-x}) \dfrac{n!}{(n-x)!x!}$

A line graph is typically used to show data that is changing continuously over time. The graph looks like a scatterplot with line segments connecting each point.

What is a bar graph?

Describe a stem-and-leaf plot.

What is the mode of a data set?

A bar graph consists of a series of vertical or horizontal bars that show the frequency of each value or category.

A stem-and-leaf plot splits each data points into a stem and a leaf, for the number twelve would be split into a stem of 1 and leaf of 2. The plot will list the leaves that correspond to each leaf.

Mode is the number that occurs most often in the set.

What is a histogram?

What is the formula for finding the probability of a single event?

What is the relationship between standard deviation and variance?

A histogram plots the frequency of quantitative data with number ranges grouped together.

$\text{probability} = \dfrac{\text{successful outcomes}}{\text{possible outcomes}}$

Standard deviation is the positive square root of variance.

What information is shown in a pie chart?

In a Venn diagram with two circles representing the probability of A and the probability of B, what is represented by the area outside the circles?

What do the terms "skewed to the left" and "skewed to the right" mean?

Pie charts show the percentages of each element of a set.

The area outside of both circles is the probability of neither A nor B.

The mean of a data set that is skewed to left is less than the median, and the mean of a data set that is skewed to the right is greater than the median.

Made in the USA
San Bernardino, CA
09 September 2017